COLD READ LIKE

A SPY

Convince Complete Strangers That You Know Everything About Them In Minutes!

By the time you've finished this book you will be able to cold read like a spy! You'll be able to walk into any bar, club or venue and instantly convince complete strangers that you know them intimately. They'll be amazed at how you seem to know their hidden traits and desires. People will think you can see directly into their mind and believe you have some kind of a power. The best of it all? It's really easy to do it and works every time.

Maybe you have seen TV programs and films where a spy seems to simply look into the eyes another person and then proceeds to tell them all about themselves, to the amazement of the person on the receiving end, always asking

"How did you know that?" Maybe you've seen mentalists and so called mind readers or these so called psychics. I hate to burst your bubble but they're not real. Or at least none that I've ever met have managed to convince me of their 'powers'. If you wish to believe in them though, that's entirely your choice. If you read on though, I'll show you how they manage to have complete strangers hanging on their every word, all because they believe what they're being told by someone who 'appears' to have some kind of a power.

I'm going to break this book down into bite size sections to make it easier to absorb and repeat what you've learned, using a method that will help commit it to your long term memory, so you are able to repeat upon demand. Any time you feel like it. I have personally used the methods I'm going to teach you, on people I'd only just met and had them telling their friends how I could 'See into their soul' and how it was 'weird but he just knew everything about me.' I've had girls saying things like 'I just felt like we were somehow connected' and 'Nobody has ever done anything like that, nobody gets me like you.' And soon you'll be hearing the same type of things too.

So who am I? My name is Gavin Stone. Author of E-books like HOW TO TRAVEL THE WORLD FOR PEANUTS. And HOW TO IMPROVE MEMORY. As well as paperback books like HOW TO TELL IF SOMEONE IS LYING. I have ghost written for other authors and also have a fiction trilogy on the way too. Please follow my Facebook page 'Gavin Stone Author' for future details, or follow me on Twitter @AuthorGavin. Thanks in advance for showing your support. My history though, differs from most. I'm a former Civil Servant for the British Ministry of Defence (M.o.D.) And previous freelance security contractor. I've worked in areas from Process Serving (or a Per-Serve as the British lawyers usually call it.) Which basically involves tracking down and serving documents (Such as a court summons) to an individual personally. Then worked my way upwards from there. When I stopped working in the field, I trained operatives that were new to the industry, in areas like Covert Surveillance, Escape & Evasion, Close Protection, Surreptitious Entry and many more. It may seem like a lot but most contracts undertaken were short term so I had to be a bit of a 'Jack of all trades, master of none'.

The part relevant to this book though was the investigations and gathering of intelligence. You may think it's all about gadgets and spying but in actual fact most of the time, the most important tool you have is your wits. You find yourself relying on favors and information from complete strangers.

Most of the time, you have to win round people who are already suspicious of you. You have to elicit information from them and they have to give it up, voluntarily. To achieve this there are several methods. All of which will depend upon your intentions towards the person you are trying to obtain information from.

There are several reasons why you might want information from a person. To find out a place where somebody lives, works or drinks frequently for example. This is when you have to make your mind up what you're going to tell the individual you are asking. The last thing you want to do is tell them you're an old school friend, only to find that the person you're talking to, went to school with them as well.

Let's assume that you've found a bar where the person you want to gain information frequents. It's now a simple matter of infiltration. In movies a spy would approach the target direct, this is to save time. In reality, you would take more time to familiarize yourself with the surroundings and the other regulars. Spot the targets friends and associates who he usually drinks with. Wait for the target to leave, then get to know his drinking buddies. Slowly but surely you gradually infiltrate and sooner or later, they will naturally introduce you to the target. You don't ask. You just wait until you're a familiar face and it will happen.

Of course this method of infiltration is one of many and would obviously change to fit the situation. In the game of investigating, dynamic assessment is my favorite term. In the instance above, this is acceptable practice to gain information on a person, if you're expecting this person to steal secrets for you however, that's a different ball game all together.

Espionage, or the stealing of secrets, involves getting a person to commit an act of betrayal. Break rules and more importantly do it without getting caught. Even more importantly for you, not getting you caught. If you get caught, your career is pretty much over. If you get them caught they face prison, being tortured or even killed. So the best way to avoid being caught is to avoid being noticed. So when you're 'spotting' (as it's called in the world of intelligence), a potential source, nobody should notice you at all. They shouldn't see you recruit them, they shouldn't see you obtaining information from them or paying or rewarding them. It's best to use what's known as a 'cut out' to act as a conduit between you and your source, or if this is not possible, utilize a dead drop method or a DLB (Dead Letter Box). That's when the old double sided tape on the envelope stuck under the park bench is used.

After you've recruited your 'Asset', nobody should be able to remember you were even there. They shouldn't remember a thing about you, be able to describe you or even be able to recall anything about you that will help to track you down. So as you can imagine, the method above is most definitely not what you'd use in a recruitment scenario. In an infiltration scenario though, it will do the job most of the time. There's a reason I have explained all of this to you, which will become more obvious later in the book.

So now we've established the differences between recruitment and infiltration we can get down to the nitty gritty. The cold reading part.

A starting point.

The first thing you need to know is that you don't need to be a spy to be able to cold read people. Anyone can do it. It's extremely easy and using the method I'm about to show you, I'm more than confident that by the end of this book you'll be easily able to do it too.

I'm going to introduce you to a system that will set the foundation for your cold read. To start with, don't waste time looking for clues. You'll see why later. There's not need to scan your target for rings or tan lines where one used to be. Notches showing on their belt or looking at their shoes, shopping bags or clothes etc. Instead you have to realize that the cold read actually happens in the person's mind, not with what you spot. It's more about the words you use that are open to interpretation of your target. Once you've said the right words, in the right way, you have set a foundation and you build from there.

People are naturally intrigued to know how the rest of the world perceives them. Which is exactly why cold reading is so powerful. A person capable of doing so, will always command the targets attention. The excitement of a person being able to tell all, has a mystery about it, which so many crave and find so appealing. It stands a chance though, that you're already aware of that. Otherwise you wouldn't be reading this book in the first place.

Section 1

So to set your foundation you simply execute what is known as a classic reading. A classic reading is simply a set of 12 stock lines. Statements that are simply truisms of the majority of people everywhere. Each of these stock lines, while being a 'one size fits all' type of statement, are delivered to the target and made to sound as if they are specific for the target alone. When delivering these stock lines you simply put them into your own words or phrase them in a way that the target believes they're about her and nobody else. (Even though these lines could apply to pretty much anyone in the world, you'd be amazed at how many times I've used them and had people in awe, believing I knew them inside out.) It's easily done when delivered the right way and I'll show you later on. The slightly harder part is committing the 12 lines to memory, and I'll help you with that too.

First though, here are the 12 lines:

1. **At times you are extroverted, affable, sociable, while at other times you are introverted, wary and reserved.**

2. You have a strong need for people to like you and for them to admire you.

3. Disciplined and controlled on the outside, you tend to be worrisome and insecure on the inside.

4. You have a tendency to be critical of yourself.

5. You pride yourself on being an independent thinker and do not accept the opinion of others without proof.

6. You have found it unwise to be frank in revealing yourself to others.

7. Your sexual side has presented some problems for you.

8. While you have some personality weaknesses, you are generally able to compensate for them.

9. At times you have serious doubts about whether you've made the right decision or done the right thing.

10. You prefer a certain amount of change and variety and become dissatisfied when hemmed in by restrictions and limitations.

11. Some of your aspirations tend to be pretty unrealistic.

12. You have a great deal of unused capacity which you have not turned to your advantage.

So the problem here is, even though there are only 12 lines, they are a bit nebulas and don't appear to be about anything. At first glance they even seem pretty familiar and most people usually remember a few but not all. Don't worry, I promised I'd help you with that and I will. I'll show you a way to cement them into your mind and recall them, as and when you need to.

You do not need to remember each line word for word. You only need to remember the concept of each line! You will need to relay these lines in your own words as you deliver them.

I will now go through each of the 12 lines individually, as well as suggesting alternatives but ultimately it's down to you to understand that the lines are fluid. Do not become a slave to the exact words. Say them in a way where the fit feels right for you.

So here we go;

LINE 1

At times you are extroverted, affable, sociable, while at other times you are introverted, wary and reserved.

To help you to remember: As a spy you live a double life. You spend a lot of time planning your next move, working out how you're going to achieve your goal, before going out there and mingling with the party guests at the embassy. The majority of people need solitude as well as socializing in regular doses. Spies are no different. So to help you to remember that, below are some alternatives you could use instead. Try to think of these as how they would relate to the world of a spy and how that crosses over to that of any other person in the world.

- Sometimes you like to plan alone, not letting people into your very secret world but after a while it can become too much and you need to get out there and mix a few drinks while you mix with a few people.

- Even though you are sociable, you like privacy time to do your own thing.

- Many people around you can see your independent side but you don't let it get in the way of family and friends.

- You appear to the world to sometimes jump straight into things but secretly you give a lot of thought and planning to most of the things you do. Or at least more than most would credit you for.

- You have fun when you want to but you need 'me time' now and again too.

- Some people may not think you have a plan but you do. You might not have thought of every angle but you know roughly how things are going to play out or where you want to end up.

LINE 2

You have a strong need for people to like you and for them to admire you.

To help you to remember: While the military have parades and recognition for their heroic work, the people of the intelligence community seldom do. When going through the selection process, one of the hardest parts for new recruits to come to terms with is the fact that they can possibly do something great but can never tell anyone. This is usually the stage where people drop out or are binned because the kind of people the intelligence agencies like to employ are the outgoing types. The ones who have that loveable rogue mixed with a salesman topping. And they're also the ones who want recognition for their achievements. People love attention and admiration. Even the quietest of people, sometimes the quietest more than any. So you can understand how it can be hard for a spy to do so much and have to keep it to themselves.

More alternatives:

- You enjoy being the center of attention but only when it suits you.

- You are proud of your achievements but this can sometimes get on peoples nerves.

- You enjoy other people's company but only when it's right for you.

- Even though you're humble mostly, you do feel there are several people who look up to you.

- You are a people person and love to be needed and don't mind the occasional sprinkling of respect either.

- You can be shy but love recognition of your hard work.

- You work hard and enjoy the praise when it's pointed out.

LINE 3

Disciplined and controlled on the outside, you tend to be worrisome and insecure on the inside.

To help you to remember: On the big screen, spies are cool, calm and collected. However, as confident as they are on the outside, it takes time, training and practice, to contain your true feelings of nerves and keep your cool in order to succeed in your task.

Alternatives:

- Most people think you glide through life effortlessly however you do have your own sets of concerns to deal with frequently.

- You can find it hard to let your guard down and let people in. To let them see the real you.

- You have learned the hard way that in order to succeed, most of the time you're better off keeping yourself to yourself.

- Revealing your emotional side has had its problems for you as you try so hard to be there for everyone else.

- No matter how hard times become, you have an inner determination that gets you through. Sometimes you amaze yourself at your own strength to cope with all the situations life throws at you.

- You usually keep your feelings contained, sometimes simply so as that you don't upset others or create unnecessary friction.

LINE 4

You have a tendency to be critical of yourself.

To help you to remember: A spy frequently has to work alone. They are left to their own devices and can use whichever methods they need to get the job done. This makes them very self-critical. They demand a lot from themselves to make sure they get their mission completed. After all, if they fail, they've only got themselves to blame. So they tend to be quite harsh with themselves. Just like many other ordinary people can too.

Alternatives:

- You can frequently worry about things going wrong and blame yourself way too often.

- You can be a bit of a perfectionist even if it doesn't seem that way to some people.

- You always hope for the best and can feel like your letting yourself down (or others) if it doesn't happen.

- You can be your own worst critic to the point of hearing praise from other people only seems like they're trying to pacify you when things don't turn out exactly how you wanted.

LINE 5

You pride yourself on being an independent thinker and do not accept the opinion of others without proof.

To help you to remember: When going out into the field, spies usually have very little information to start out with. They have to work independently to obtain intelligence and build a bigger picture of their own. They soon learn that not everyone can be trusted. This is what leads them to finding out the facts for themselves, instead of taking what's written in a report as being 100% truthful. A spy's independent thinking is key to finding out those facts.

Alternatives:

- You can be a good listener but still like to make your own mind up about what really happened.

- Knowing what really happened to you is important but can also land you in trouble at times.

- You have a need to know the truth and won't just blindly follow others.

- You're not easily convinced and need to come to conclusions on your own.

- You can appear stubborn and headstrong at times but this is only because you need evidence to validate new information and don't just take things at face value.

- You can have a sense of pride that can occasionally get in the way of rational thinking.

- You don't just get a piece of new information and go with it, you like to mull things over and conclude things by yourself and in your own time.

- You are happy to take in new information but won't necessarily believe it to be set in stone as truth, until you've had it validated by trusted sources.

LINE 6

You have found it unwise to be frank in revealing yourself to others.

To help you to remember: Spies frequently work under cover. Mostly they are under the cover of a diplomat but occasionally they are in the most precarious of situations and have to perform under what's known as Non-Official Cover (N.O.C.). This gives them zero diplomatic protection and therefor they have to be more cautious than ever. As you can imagine, the last thing you want is to be regularly revealing to people that you're a spy.

If you gave that kind of information out to ever girl you jumped into bed with, then you'd be telling about 19 people a week. (Or there abouts), but you get the picture. The more people who know, the more vulnerable you become, so you don't just blab to everyone that you meet, that you're a spy. As I'm sure you can imagine. Just like the majority of the world don't walk around telling people their vulnerabilities.

Alternatives:

- You have a lot going on underneath the surface, however it's only the people you feel comfortable with sharing, that know this side of you.

- In the past you've let people in too soon and learned the hard way that not everyone can be trusted, leading you to regret it later on.

- Over all you're quite an open person but you've learned to be cautious with it.

- You've learned through experience it's not always wise to wear your heart on your sleeve.

- You have had your fair share of setbacks from people you thought you could trust, so now you choose more carefully who you reveal you're true thoughts and fears to.

- You sometimes mask who you really are until you learn

whether you can really trust a person or not.

LINE 7

Your sexual side has presented some problems for you.

To help you to remember: During the Cold War, the Russians trained female operatives to be a seductress, in order to obtain intelligence from the Americans. They were known as Swallows. The Germans also had a male version that the CIA referred to as Romeos. I'm sure there's plenty of spy films you have seen where the hero is seduced by a female counterpart or where the hero has seduced her in order to get what he wants. It happens frequently in all areas of life. On many occasions I've had to at least flirt with someone in order to achieve my objective.

Alternatives:

- Your love life has confused you in the past. Figuring out the opposite sex has not been without challenges.

- You want to be loved by someone who loves you on the same level and find previously either someone has loved you and you don't quiet feel the same or you're the one doing all the loving.

- It's taken you some time to get to grips with how to express yourself to the opposite sex.

- You sometimes want to show your true emotions but experience has taught you to tread carefully in how fast you say how you really feel.

- The opposite sex has been a bit of a mystery to you in the past but you're finally figuring out how to play the game.

- You have been subject to heartbreak in the past but are learning how to use knowledge of the opposite sex to your advantage.

LINE 8

While you have some personality weaknesses, you are generally able to compensate for them.

To help you to remember: Spies have to undergo frequent Psyc-evals or psychic evaluations, in order to determine their suitability to continue working in the field, (among other things). To the outside world they have to appear to be the epitome of perfection, so when areas of weakness arise, they have to play up to their strengths in order to camouflage any weak spots until they're worked on and strengthened.

Alternatives:

- Nobody's perfect but you can sometimes find it hard to admit your own faults.

- There are areas that you wish you were more talented in and this can sometimes distract you from seeing some of your own strengths.

- Sometimes you can give yourself a hard time, even over things that are out of your control, yet you know there are so many areas of your life, where you more than make up for the occasional silly little mistake.

- You can spend hours dedicating your attention to something you love but have a tendency to hastily get things that annoy you out of the way and done.

- You can be compulsive sometimes over things you like or really want but have the restraint and mental strength to use it when you want to.

- You do so many good things in your life but still tend to worry sometimes about insignificant imperfections.

- Sometimes you stress over things that nobody would notice other than you, yet you know in the

grand scheme of things they're
not that relevant.

- You have so much talent in so
  many areas, yet sometimes you
  can be so tough on yourself for
  the smallest of mistakes, even
  blowing them out of proportion at
  times.

LINE 9

At times you have serious doubts about whether you've made the right decision or done the right thing.

To help you to remember: Being a spy can regularly have you facing conflicted choices. It can be impossibly difficult to choose between what you believe to be morally right and what you need to do for the greater good. When confronted with these decisions so often, spies frequently ask themselves a particular question. 'Was being a spy the right choice for me?' Every spy has asked themselves this at least once in their career (whether they admit it or not). This is their human side that doesn't get seen very often. Although when you get the next call to tell you what you have to do this time, you forget all that and get back to work.

Alternatives:

- Sometimes you question your choices but you carry on regardless.

- You worry sometimes about past events reaping themselves in the future.

- Sometimes you wonder why other people's lives seem to be so easy in comparison to yours and ask yourself if you've chosen the right path.

- You haven't always made the best choices in the past and this sometimes affects you in the present when it comes to making choices in the here and now.

- You can reflect a little too much on the past sometimes.

- Sometimes you look around you and wonder if you have made the right decisions in your life.

- You sometimes wish you could go back to the past, knowing what you know now.

- You have learned so much on your life that you sometimes think you should be doing things differently.

LINE 10

You prefer a certain amount of change and variety and become dissatisfied when hemmed in by restrictions and limitations.

To help you to remember: If I had a dollar for every time a spy had defied orders, I'd probably never need to work again. Working in the field trumps any office position, any day of the week. You have a real time view of every situation around you and therefore have the ability to override the orders of the person giving them. You are the one calling the shots and ultimately you get to say what goes. Like any other person, nobody likes being told what to do.

Alternatives:

- Sometimes you have to go against what others might see as right or wrong in order to make sure people don't get hurt.

- You have always done things in an unconventional way but not in a way that might be extremely obvious.

- Your feeling of freedom is important to you and you don't feel comfortable being told what you can and can't do.

- At times of you feeling miserable, it's mostly because you feel trapped in some way or another and this occasionally makes you think back to times of when you had your freedom.

- You have a rebellious streak but also maintain the ability to keep your cool when needed.

LINE 11

Some of your aspirations tend to be pretty unrealistic.

To help you to remember: What happens in spy movies in comparison to what happens in real life situations is extremely different. As a spy, you're actually a small cog in a big machine that helps gather information for people further up the chain to make decisions. What they decide to then present to people further up the chain then gets filtered into what is imminently important. Eventually, this information (if important enough) makes its way to the decision makers and they decide whether to act upon it or not. Although to the spy in the field, what they're doing is going to save the world (in their eyes).

Alternatives:

- You sometimes set yourself goals that you know you can't reach in reality right now but would love to one day achieve.

- You've learned the hard way, that sometimes, trying to be someone you're not doesn't work out to well but you don't give up trying to improve yourself.

- You dream of a better future that sometimes distracts you from the here and now.

- Your hopes for the future can occasionally take you away from living in the moment.

- You have done your fair share of wishful thinking but something tells you that you're not set for the same destiny as most other people.

LINE 12

You have a great deal of unused capacity which you have not turned to your advantage.

To help you to remember: When going through the training process, spies are often expected to go above and beyond. They sometimes amaze themselves at their own abilities to think outside or the box or react to unprecedented situations. They are trained to realize how much of life is about mind-set and how sometimes, the most hopeless of situations can turn around when they go back to their training and just look at things from a different angle. Their training is designed to make them realize their hidden abilities. Sometimes, in the tightest of situations, a spy has one more trick left when they're backed into a corner.

Alternatives:

- You have so many talents you have yet to fully embrace.

- You can drive your friends and family to frustration when they can see the potential within you, even when you might be blissfully unaware of it.

- I feel you have so many abilities that you are waiting to reveal until the time is right.

- I think you get frustrated when you have so many ideas and can't focus on any of them because of your current circumstances.

- You can be a giving person but you have so much more to give if you could just unlock some of your potential talents.

- Sometimes you can be so caught up in the moment that you forget exactly how resourceful you can be.

- You have yet to realize how many talents lay dormant within you. You know some of them are there and unused but there's so much

more to you than most people
see.

So there are your 12 stock lines. I will also tell you how to go further in manipulating your target into thinking you know everything about them later on but for now, as promised, I'm going to help you commit these lines to memory, so you can recall them as and when you need to. In order for this to work, I need you visualize places in your mind that you know extremely well and we will set those places to create a vivid picture in your mind for each line. These pictures will help create a bridge between your short term and long term memory (For more details about bridging the gap between short term and long term memory, get a copy of my E-book HOW TO IMPROVE MEMORY from Amazon now). So, we are going to create some exceptionally vivid and farfetched images in your mind to help you lock each of these lines in your mind to grab from your 'toolbox' as and when you need them. So here we go.

1) You're sitting at home when the wall slides upwards to reveal a screen. The screen lights up and your boss (a director at one of the world's biggest spy agencies), tells you they have a mission for you. You have to go to the embassy and attend a party. While you are there you have to achieve a task that only you can do! This brings us to line one:

At times you are extroverted, affable, sociable, while at other times you are introverted, wary and reserved.

You begin to make your plan and work out what you're going to do when you're at the embassy drinking vodka martinis amongst the other guests.

2) You go to your wardrobe to pick out the best outfit for the occasion. Your only real goal is to complete your mission but you want to enjoy the party while you're there and you certainly don't want anyone judging you from your attire, if anything you

want to be found attractive or even envied.

You have a strong need for people to like you and for them to admire you.

3) After dressing in your best clothes, you mentally prepare yourself for you mission. A cool steely exterior keeps anyone from suspecting you're really there with ulterior motives.

Disciplined and controlled on the outside, you tend to be worrisome and insecure on the inside.

4) Working alone you know you have to get this right. There are no margins for error and you check your appearance in the mirror.

You have a tendency to be critical of yourself.

You brush the slightest of white marks from your shoulder and adjust your clothes one last time before you head to the party. When you get there, you scan the room to double check that the information you've been given about the layout matches with how it actually is.

You pride yourself on being an independent thinker and do not accept the opinion of others without proof.

5) After a quick scan you spot a beautiful young lady walking across the room towards you.

   You have found it unwise to be frank in revealing yourself to others.

   You don't want to blow your cover at this point so you keep your cool and wait to see what she says before you react.

6) You have no diplomatic protection and are an NOC so you have to be more cautious than ever.

   Your sexual side has presented some problems for you.

You know in the past, Russians have used Swallows and other intelligence agencies have trained operatives to use seduction as a weapon. You are more careful in choosing who you open up to.

Your sexual side has presented some problems for you.

7) You know from previous mistakes how that could go so you keep your guard up. She asks you for a light and you oblige. She then offers you a cigarette.

While you have some personality weaknesses,

**you are generally able to
compensate for them.**

8) You refuse and chew on some
   gum instead. You have your habits
   but your abilities to override them
   and do better is there when it
   counts.

**At times you have serious doubts
about whether you've made the
right decision or done the right
thing.**

9) She walks away and leaving you to
   reflect on your decisions. You
   begin to question your previous
   choices. Maybe you should have
   settled with someone nice like
   that years ago. You ask yourself
   'was being a spy the right choice

for me?' You snap out of it and remember you've got orders.

You prefer a certain amount of change and variety and become dissatisfied when hemmed in by restrictions and limitations.

10)   Breaking away from your thoughts, your attention is thrusted to yet another stunning person walking into the room. You are in a position where you can ignore your orders. You can make a 'boots on the ground' decision. You could tell them it all went pear shaped if you wanted and just spend the night with the

gorgeous looker who just strolled in.

Some of your aspirations tend to be pretty unrealistic.

11)   You watch as the hot prospect walks over, drink in hand. You have your dreams of where you'd love the conversation to go but you also remember, you have to save the world.

You have a great deal of unused capacity which you have not turned to your advantage.

12)   She tells you she has keys to the office where you want to plant a listening device. Then goes on to tell you that her friend whose cigarette you lit wants to come with you both upstairs to the locked office. Blam! Two birds, one stone. You've reached that level of hidden potential that you knew was deep inside you all the time. You've surpassed your expectations. You get to complete your mission and have two gorgeous girls by your side as you do it!

So the reason I set this little scenario out for you is to help to commit it to your memory. When the time comes to recall it, you simply replay this little sequence of actions in your head and you will be able to verbally regurgitate everything you've just read. Don't get me wrong, you may not do it word perfect but that's exactly what I'm relying on. When you're in a position that makes you word it your way on the spot, it looks so much more authentic. It looks like you're finding the words to describe the individual you're talking to and not just reeling off stock lines. Ultimately making you even more believable.

A little side note: Don't worry of someone says 'no that doesn't apply to me'. Just gloss over it and carry on with the next line. I'll explain more about how and why you'll get away with this later in the book.

Section 2

The Application process

This is where we start to explore the ways you can convince your target that you can see into their soul. The whole thing revolves around telling them what they want to hear and moving swiftly past any blips that might occur along the way.

First of all you have to diffuse the notion that you reading is in any way a challenge. Once you've used the stock lines to grab their interest, you then want to reel them in. You tell them that if they want more, (which they always will) they have to understand it's a two way exchange. You need them to display openness and honesty in order for your reading to be successful. All the time emphasizing that this two way process only works if they're being completely truthful and open.

With your hints of the reading only being successful with the targets complete cooperation, this primes the target to be as helpful as they can be. After all nobody wants to be a failure. In all truth, deep down they want you to succeed. After all, who doesn't want to be told a bunch of nice things about themselves?

The priority though is simply to ensure that the target understands that this is an 'open dialogue'. By letting your target know at this stage that the reading is a joint effort, you've opened up a whole new world of possibilities and any preconceived notions that the whole process revolves around everything you say, instantly evaporates.

This is the point where you back track slightly. Even though these stock lines fit the majority of the world's population, countless times I have had people believing that the statement was solely about them. Your description was so accurate of their personality they convince themselves that you could only have ever said these words to them. They are the ones at this point selling it to themselves. All you've got to do now is continue down the path of agreeing they couldn't possibly be wrong.

Here's how you do it. You've already got them in what I like to call 'nodding dog' mode. They're excited and enjoying it, so they want to hear more. This is when they'll begin to only hear the things they like. Their mind will literally filter out anything that doesn't apply to them and only absorb the bits that fit. All the time smiling and saying to you 'yes, you're right' and similar phrases. Then the inevitable question comes; "How do you know all this stuff about me?" This where your 'Cold Reading' skills come in. Remember earlier when I told you not to look for clues?

There's no need. The stock lines were enough to open the door and convince the target you know them intimately but you can now use props if you really want to.

You can now say things like: "Looking at your clothes and carefully observing you physiology, I'd say you're a pretty happy go lucky person on the exterior. I reckon most people think you're an out there, fun loving type. However, looking at your purse, that says something a little different. It's more conservative in its design. As nice as it is, it's not coming close to the level of wild you seem to have on most nights out, or even some of the fun I watched you having here earlier tonight. I get the impression that you're actually a lot more reserved than people perceive you to be and can actually be a bit worrier on occasions. This re-enforces that you are actually cold reading the person. Now you can ramp it up a notch.

Remember, you don't have to rehearse these lines so they come out smoothly every time. It's actually better if they're a bit clunky. It looks more authentic if the person believes you're speaking as you observe all the details about them. In a lot of instances, pauses and short silences can be your best friend. It makes it look like you are calculating from your observations. It also gives the target chance to fill in the gaps themselves. I've known subjects who have told the 'Cold Reader' more than the reader has told them and walked away amazed at how he knew them so intimately. So if the target starts waffling on about themselves, let them carry on. Just sit there nodding and agreeing, they're doing the hard work for you.

In a social setting this can work even better sometimes. For example, if you find yourself sitting amongst a group of 5 or 6 girls and you're giving one of them a 'reading', you will find a lot of the time, their friends will also help fill in the gaps. I've done it before, where girls around the table start saying things like: "Oh my gosh, that's so you" or "Yes, you do that kind of thing all the time, that's so true." It can be a real help. The one thing you have got to be aware of though, is that when you've finished with one girl, you can guarantee the next on will say: "Do me!" Which will be followed by "Me next." The main problem with this, is if you've used up all of your 12 stock lines, you will have to think really hard of ways to rephrase them for the next subject that sounds completely different and yet is still telling them the same thing. My advice here would be to use 2 or 3 lines on each of them to get them hooked, then move to the next level. Which I'm going to teach you about next.

Shifting it up a gear.

So now we're at the point where you've used the stock lines to create the interest. You've given a small demonstration of how you deduce these facts and got the 'nodding dog' affect. This is where your subject comes into play. People love to talk about themselves. Some more than others but everyone's favorite subject is them self. This is where you cash in.

When you start getting a string of agreements, with some sort of information thrown in (which will happen more often than you can imagine) you should give the impression that you already knew that all along and they were in fact continuing with *your* train of thought, not the other way around.

Let's say for instance you've made a statement like "You have a tendency to look back at your past a little more often than is good for you." And they respond by giving you a snippet of information about a recent ex they haven't quite got over yet, You just carry on with "Yes, And I also get the feeling you're finding it a struggle to adjust to being single again." By continuing without blinking, it appears that knew about their recent break up and that they were only agreeing with something you were saying to them. Not the other way around. It may sound obvious but it works seamlessly all the time.

The tiny snippet of information they volunteered can now be used to go a step further and convince them even more that you have an ability to connect with them like no other person on the planet. You know they're looking at moving on so you simply say something along the lines of the following:

"I can tell by your posture that you're naturally a strong and determined person. Your inner strength and attitude is what's going to take you to a new chapter in your life. A new beginning that will allow you to let go of all the baggage that's been holding you back for so long. It may feel a little scary going into the unknown alone and you may feel as if you're not quite ready but as this new start in your life is on the horizon, you are so near to being your stronger self. A little more persistence and you'll definitely have a brighter future. You've got what it takes!"

It might seem like a lot to take in and repeat but the truth is simple, when you ask yourself an even simpler question. What have I really said? All I've done it given them a bit of a positive pep talk, tell them something they'd like to hear and bingo. She's already told me where the problem area is (getting over her ex) which of course I 'already knew'. All I did was tell her she's going to get over it in a nice way and she's happy. All of the stock lines and that kind of nebulous stuff will be forgotten and the only thing she will remember, will be that 'YOU TOLD HER' that she's had a recent break up, she'll soon be over her relationship problems, she's going to get her life and track and of course because you were so spot on and right about all of the other stuff, why wouldn't you be right when you added that she's got a bright future coming too?

A small adage here is to not come across as gushing and just spewing out niceties that people love to hear. In order to come across as sincere you need to bring it down to earth now and again with a couple of red flags and realisms. Try dropping a few warnings in there, which can be anything that will apply to a recently separated girl. Say things like: "This time try looking at your past choices in men and telling yourself some honest truths." Or "Avoid the men that rides motorbikes." If you want to be a little more specific. (For the record here, I don't have anything against men who ride bikes, it was simply an example you could use.) This small statement alone could spark off a whole new set of reactions. Her friends might say, "Oh, your ex had a bike." Or "Hey, that guy who was chatting you up at the coffee shop every lunch break has a bike." If you want to go the other way, tell her to look for something specific. Colors are always a good thing to use here. Like: "Look for a man in a red car." Or a particular job. "I see you settling with a successful realtor." The more common the job the better.

I've used instances here where the subject it female but these same kind of methods work on males just as easily. Only you may have to seem to have made an observation about their shoes, rather than their purse. Pointing out their clothes or hardened hands, workers posture etc. All of these things will achieve the desired affect.

As you can see, it's reasonably easy to have a subject convinced that you know all about them. One of the main keys here is confidence. Don't blink. Even if you get something wrong, dismiss it and move on. They won't remember the bits you got wrong, they will filter that out. They'll vividly remember things that you appeared to tell them though, that were hard facts. Remember when you deliver your lines that the person listening will automatically connect what you're telling them with their own circumstances or life. It's down to you to connect these dots and emphasize by repeating back to them the facts that they have actually told you. By doing this you come across as being the one to have known all the details and it was you who not only knew the hard facts all along but that you told them and they said nothing and gave nothing away. It happens all the time.

If on the off chance one of the stock lines doesn't fit your target, simply gloss over it and carry on with the next one. Make out as if you were trying to work something out about them and your thoughts trailed off slightly, so you weren't wrong, you were just thinking out loud. Don't push it or press the issue, simply brush past it and move on. The alternative is to re-frame the concept of what you said in a way that implies the target has simply misinterpreted what you have said. Don't take blame, don't say thing like "oh, my bad" Or "Sorry, I maybe explained that wrong". Just say something like: "No, what I meant was...." And then maybe choose one of the key components from your last phrase that would most definitely be a truism for anyone and emphasize that one.

SECTION 3

So now you've learned about how to use stock lines, how to rotate a conversation to make it look like you've told them everything and they've given nothing away, now I'm going to give you a little method to assist you in eliciting information from them. When you've reached the level of achieving the nodding dog affect, you occasionally insert what's known as a 'double negative' question.

An example of a double negative question is this:

"You don't have a cat do you?"

No matter what the subject answers, there's no way you have got this wrong! If they answer 'No' you simply say, "I didn't think so." and move on. If they answer 'Yes' Then you say, "I thought as much." And now you have more data to work with. You know more about this person that you can extrapolate as you continue. (I've found it best here to use a cat when talking to a female and a dog when talking to a male. This is not a sexist system, it's just based on odds and percentages.)

Double negative questions are a failsafe but should be used sparingly! You should never lead with them, always start with stock lines, you only use them after you've got the subject in a state of compliance (Nodding Dog). More importantly, you only pop them in here and there between statements and stock lines. That way if you're not on the mark you can swiftly gloss and move on. If you're right you can achieve the 'How did you know?" factor once again to leave the target in a sense of amazement at your uncanny abilities.

Remember, this is only a way of eliciting information from your target. If you don't get it right, it tells you something about them and you can move on and come back to that piece of information later if need be, or if you got it spot on, you can choose to elaborate later or then and there if you feel the need. A simple, "I had you down as an animal lover, I deduced it was a cat by the tiny occasional claw marks that are barely visible at the bottom of your jeans." Or something along those lines. They may look down, where one of two things will happen, they will either see them, or convince themselves that they see them and say "Oh yeah." Or they won't see them but won't want to look a fool so will ignore it and move on.

There are other statements you can make that are also truisms. Like: "Something tells me you have travel plans on the horizon." A wonderful statement that is again true of everyone. Everyone has travel plans. The key word here is 'plans'. Just because you plan something, doesn't mean you're actually doing it or going to do it. Travel doesn't necessarily mean vacation either. It could be travelling to work, a road trip, a family visit and so many more. People travel every day. The plans part of it takes things even further. I know people who have been planning to go away for a break for years. If you ask, you'll find there are a fair amount of people that have intentions of going on vacation somewhere soon. It may seem vague but it is exactly what I said it was; a travel plan.

There are plenty more truisms you can use. I could list them in this book but that would end up making it more of a dictionary of statements, rather than teaching you what's a relatively easy concept. You can google them if you're struggling to work out any of your own. The main purpose of this book is not to tell you what to say but teach you the simplicity in the methodology behind cold reading.

In Conclusion

This brings us to the end of your lessons in cold reading, it's probably changed your perception a little of how it all works and maybe even surprised you that it's not done the way most people think it is. Using the spy analogies should have helped you to remember ways to replay the scenario for you to repeat what you've learned easily enough and deliver a convincing cold read. One of the most important things for you to remember is confidence!

Be confident under fire. No matter what, Keep your cool and press on. Remember, they want to believe you, they want you to get it right. They want to hear nice things about themselves. It inflates the ego and makes them feel good, sooner or later you'll get it spot on and the same effect will be achieved. They'll think you know everything about them. Most of the time they'll help you out by telling you more than you're telling them, so leave the pauses, let them fill the gaps and carry on like you said it. When they tell their friends, they'll be saying you told them, not they told you.

Now that you know the basics of cold reading go out and give it a try. Ask a stranger at the coffee shop if they mind you trying to voice an observation. Curiosity will make most people want to know what you've observed about them. This gives you a chance to start off with your first try on a complete stranger. They will either love it or be a little bemused, either way, don't let anything deter you or make you too cocky. Whatever the result, learn from it and move on the next person. I'm not suggesting you sit in the coffee shop all day giving people cold reads by the way. Change places, use different venues over several days until you get enough practice to feel confident in your delivery. Once you have reached a great level of confidence, get friends of yours to introduce you to friends of theirs and watch as they become amazed at your ability to read them like a book. When you've seen how easy it actually is, you'll want to buy all of my other books!

I'd love your feedback on this short book and if you want to show your appreciation, then reviews mean an awful lot to any author. Feel free to follow me on Twitter @AuthorGavin and Like my Facebook page Gavin Stone Author, to stay up to date with new releases. Thank you.

Printed in Great Britain
by Amazon

17051661R00059